MEL BAY PRESENTS

A BASIC GUIDE

by COREY CHRISTIANSEN

1 2 3 4 5 6 7 8 9 0

Rock Scales

The **Gig Savers**™ series has been designed to give aspiring guitarists answers to common questions in a brief, affordable, yet informative fashion. This volume deals with the scales that are most commonly used in all styles of rock and roll and popular music. Most rock guitarists use only a few scales when they are soloing and building melodies. This is great because just about anyone with a reasonable IQ can learn how to use these scales. There are many scales that are used in music, but if you are just getting started, the scales in this book are the best place to begin. Each scale will be presented on fretboard diagrams showing the fingerings for each scale. A brief discussion on how to use the scale will follow. Let's get started.

The root (R) is the letter name of a scale or chord. Since the fingerings on the following page show where the root note is, the fingerings are moveable. This means that by positioning the scale shapes in different locations, each scale may be played in any key. For convenience, charts showing the root notes on each string of the guitar have been provided below. Remember, to flat a note, simply move it down (toward the nut of the guitar) one fret. To sharp a note, simply move the note one fret higher (toward the body of the guitar).

Root Notes on the Sixth and First Strings

Fret	0	1	3	5	7	8	10	12
Root Name	E	F	G	A	B	C	D	E

Root Notes on the Fifth String

Fret	0	2	3	5	7	8	10	12
Root Name	A	B	C	D	E	F	G	A

Root Notes on the Fourth String

Fret	0	2	3	5	7	9	10	12
Root Name	D	E	F	G	A	B	C	D

Root Notes on the Third String

Fret	0	2	4	5	7	9	10	12
Root Name	G	A	B	C	D	E	F	G

Root Notes on the Second String

Fret	0	1	3	5	6	8	10	12
Root Name	B	C	D	E	F	G	A	B

Minor Pentatonic Scale

The minor pentatonic scale is the Holy Grail of rock scales. As the name implies, it uses five notes (penta) to complete an octave. Everyone from Jimi Hendrix and Jimmy Page to Steve Vai and Jeff Beck have used it at one time or another. It is a scale everyone must know to play rock guitar. Here are the fingerings.

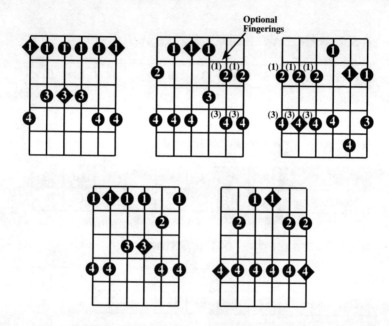

Of course this scale can be used against minor chords that have the same letter name as the scale (A minor pentatonic over an Am chord), as well as the chord progressions created from minor keys. It can also be used against dominant seventh chords that have the same letter name as well all the chords in the 12-bar blues (I-IV-V). Once you find out the tonal center of a chord progression in the typical rock song, pentatonic scales can be used over all the chords. In other words, the scale doesn't have to change every time the chord does. This is why many rock guitarists love this scale. There doesn't have to be a lot of thinking involved once you learn the scale. Just mix up the notes creatively and melodically to make up a solo. Experiment with this scale. Here are a few applications for the minor pentatonic scale.

Use A minor pentatonic to solo over these chords.

Use G minor pentatonic to solo over these chords.

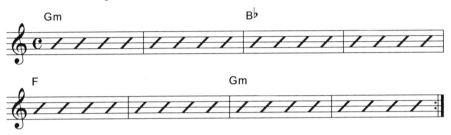

Remember, in rock music, power chords are used in place of "full" chords*. Power chords are neither major nor minor in quality. One would play the same power chord for Gm and G major. Power Chords are written with the number 5 (G5, A5, etc.). For the purposes of this book, full chords have been written out for the chord progressions. Each guitarist should try the chord progressions by playing power chords (check out "Gig Savers Power Chords").

Knowing the chords that go together in every key can assist in knowing which scales to use over a set of chord changes. For more information about this subject, check out "Gig Savers-Power Chords" and "Gig Savers-Barre Chords".

***Note:** Power chords (A5, G5, etc.) can substitute for any of the major or minor chords presented.

Major Pentatonic Scale

The minor pentatonic scale's brother is the major pentatonic. It is commonly used against major chords and the chord progressions that are made from major keys. Here are the fingerings.

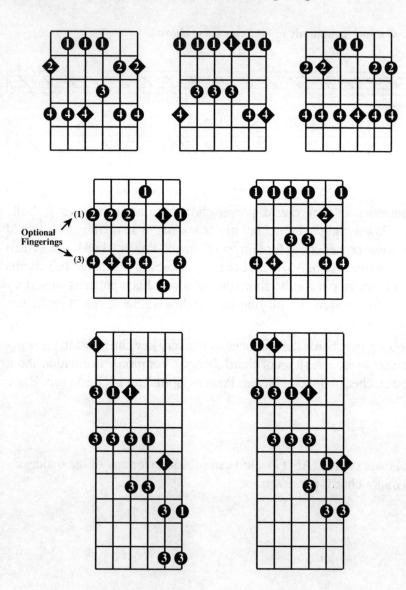

Here are chord progressions that the major pentatonic scale will work over. Experiment using this scale over other chord progressions as well.

Use G major pentatonic to solo over these chords.

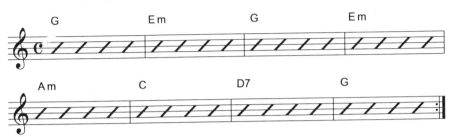

Use D major pentatonic to solo over these chords.

Relative Major and Minor

Every major scale has a relative minor scale and vice versa. This means that the notes that make up a major scale can also be used to make up a different minor scale. Examining the similarities in the fingering diagrams for both scales will prove this point. This means that a relative minor scale shape may be played where a major scale was traditionally used. By understanding this principal, every guitarist will have double the ammunition when playing solos over chord progressions.

To figure out the relative minor for a major scale, simply move one and a half steps (three frets) lower. The relative minor for C major is A minor. To find the relative major for a minor scale, simply move one and a half steps higher. The relative major of D minor is F major. The chart below shows the relative major and minor for all twelve keys. Experiment playing the major pentatonic scale over the relative minor chord and vice versa.

Major	Minor
A	F♯m
B♭	Gm
B	G♯m
C	Am
D♭	B♭m
D	Bm
E♭	Cm
E	C♯m
F	Dm
G♭	E♭m
G	Em
A♭	Fm

The Blues Scale

As the name implies, the blues scale can be used to solo over any blues progression. (Remember, the blues progression is the grandfather of all American pop music.) The blues scale can also be used just about everywhere the minor pentatonic scale is used. It differs from the minor pentatonic scale in that it has one added note. The fingerings for this scale are shown below.

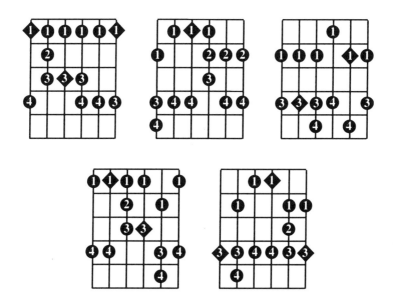

Here are a couple of twelve-bar blues progressions. Notice that the first chord in the blues determines which blues scale to use. (Use the C blues scale for blues progressions in the key of C and the G blues scale for blues progressions in the key of G.)

Use the G blues scale to solo over this progression.

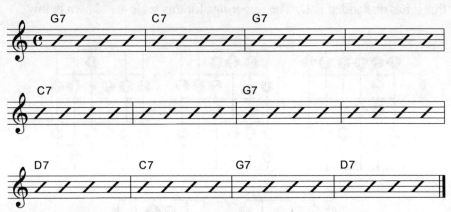

Use the C blues scale to solo over this progression.

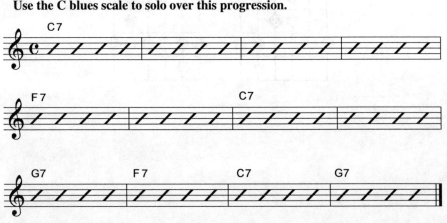

Natural and Harmonic Minor Scale

Two other minor scales that are commonly used are the natural minor and harmonic minor scale. The only difference between these two scales is the harmonic minor scale has a raised seventh degree. For the most part, these two scales can be played where the minor pentatonic scale is used. Each guitarist's ears will let him or her know whether or not the harmonic minor scale should be used. This scale has a very distinct sound and should be used carefully in minor chord progressions.

Natural Minor Scale

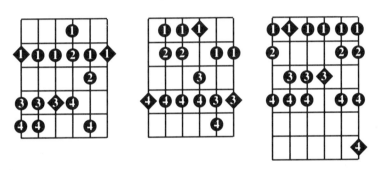

Harmonic Minor Scale

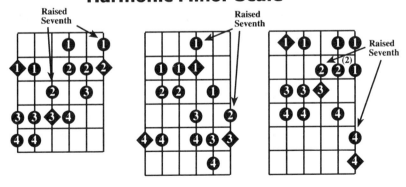

Scalar Patterns

A great way to gain speed, accuracy and become more familiar with a scale is by practicing and playing scalar patterns. A scalar pattern is simply a repeated pattern of notes through a scale. Because many people find it easier to organize and sequence numbers than notes in a scale, numbers are assigned to every note in any scale. Shown below is a minor pentatonic scale with numbers assigned to each note.

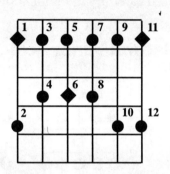

Make up any two to four number pattern such as: 1-2-3, 2-3-4, 3-4-5, etc. (Smaller numbers are easier at first.) Now that a pattern has been formulated, plug in the notes assigned to the numbers. Each pattern can be played in reverse order (5-4-3, 4-3-2, 3-2-1). The combinations are limitless. Use this technique with every new scale learned. This is a great trick to plug into any solo. A few numerical sequences have been provided below to help students get started.

Forward		Reverse	
	1-3, 2-4, 3-5, 4-6, etc.		6-4, 5-3, 4-2, 3-1
	1-2-3-4, 2-3-4-5, 3-4-5-6 etc.		6-5-4-3, 5-4-3-2, 4-3-2-1
	1-2-3, 2-3-4, 4-5-6 etc.		6-5-4, 5-4-3, 4-3-2, 3-2-1
	1-2-1-2, 3-4-3-4, 5-6-5-6 etc.		6-5-6-5, 4-3-4-3, 2-1-2-1

The Major Scale

The major scale is basically the mother of all scales. It is used in virtually every style of music on earth. It can be used to create solos and melodies over major chords with the same letter name as the scale. It can also be used to solo over any of the chords derived from a major key. A complete chart showing all of the chords in each key is shown below.

I Major	ii Minor	iii Minor	IV Major	V Major	vi Minor	vii° Diminished
C	Dm	Em	F	G	Am	Bdim
F	Gm	Am	B♭	C	Dm	Edim
B♭	Cm	Dm	E♭	F	Gm	Adim
E♭	Fm	Gm	A♭	B♭	Cm	Ddim
A♭	B♭m	Cm	D♭	E♭	Fm	Gdim
D♭	E♭m	Fm	G♭	A♭	B♭m	Cdim
G♭	A♭m	B♭m	C♭	D♭	E♭m	Fdim
B	C♯m	D♯m	E	F♯	G♯m	A♯dim
E	F♯m	G♯m	A	B	C♯m	D♯dim
A	Bm	C♯m	D	E	F♯m	G♯dim
D	Em	F♯m	G	A	Bm	C♯dim
G	Am	Bm	C	D	Em	F♯dim

Here are a number of fingerings for the major scale.

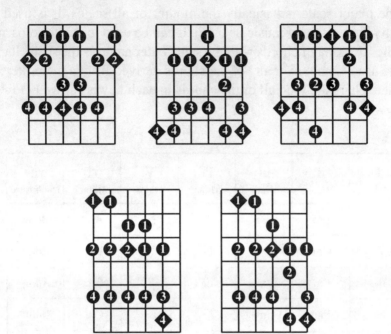

Modes
The Dorian Mode

Modes are simply scales that are derived from another scale. The Dorian mode is the scale that is built from the second degree of the major scale. This means that the D Dorian mode contains the same notes as the C major scale, but the tonal center is D. It is minor in quality, which makes it an excellent choice when soloing over minor, m7, m9, m7sus, and m6 chords. This scale can also be thought of as a natural minor scale with a raised sixth degree. This is the scale that Santana used when soloing over *Oye Como Va*.

Here are some fingerings for the Dorian mode.

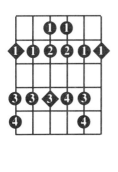 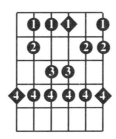 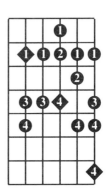

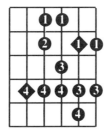

The Mixolydian Mode

The Mixolydian mode is the scale built from the fifth degree of the major scale. This means that the G Mixolydian mode and the C major scale contain the same notes, they just have a different tonal center. The Mixolydian mode can also be thought of as a major scale with a flatted seventh degree. The Mixolydian mode is an excellent choice when soloing over dominant seventh (7th) chords. However, when dominant seventh chords change, the mode must be changed also. For example, if a chord progression has the chords G7 and C7, the G Mixolydian mode should be used over G7 and the C Mixolydian mode should be used over the C7.

Here are some fingerings for the Mixolydian mode.

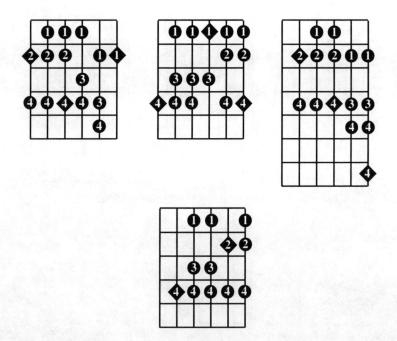